Let's go by

Barbara Hunter

Heinemann

Little Nippers

www.heinemann.co.uk/library
Visit our website to find out more information about **Heinemann Library** books.

To order:
☎ Phone 44 (0) 1865 888066
▤ Send a fax to 44 (0) 1865 314091
▯ Visit the Heinemann Bookshop at www.heinemann.co.uk/library to browse our catalogue and order online.

First published in Great Britain by Heinemann Library, Halley Court, Jordan Hill, Oxford OX2 8EJ, part of Harcourt Education.
Heinemann is a registered trademark of Harcourt Education Ltd.

Editorial: Jilly Attwood and Claire Throp
Design: Jo Hinton-Malivoire and bigtop, Bicester, UK
Models made by: Jo Brooker
Picture Research: Lodestone Publishing Limited
Production: Lorraine Warner

Originated by Dot Gradations
Printed and bound in China by South China Printing Company

ISBN 0 431 16463 0 (hardback)
06 05 04 03 02
10 9 8 7 6 5 4 3 2 1

ISBN 0 431 16468 1 (paperback)
06 05 04 03 02
10 9 8 7 6 5 4 3 2 1

British Library Cataloguing in Publication Data
Hunter, Barbara
Let's go by car
388.3'2
A full catalogue record for this book is available [from the Britis]h Library.

[Acknowledg]ements
[The publishers] would like to thank the following [for permission] to reproduce photographs:
[Art Directo]rs pp. **6**, **16**, **18**, **19**; Bubbles p. **7a** [(Jennie Woodcock]); Collections p. **15** (Peter Wright); [Sally an]d Greenhill Photo Library p. **10** [(Sally Greenhil]l), p. **20-21** (Richard Greenhill); Sylvia Cordaiy Photo Library p. **17** (Humphrey Evans); Tografox pp. **4-5**, **7b**, **8**, **9**, **11**, **12-13**, **14** (R. D. Battersby).

Cover photograph reproduced with permission of PA Photos (Phil Noble).

The publishers would like to thank Annie Davy for her assistance in the preparation of this book.

Every effort has been made to contact copyright holders of any material reproduced in this book. Any omissions will be rectified in subsequent printings if notice is given to the publishers.

Contents

Journeys

Where did you go on your last car journey?

Where do you think these people are going?

Why do people go by car?

Shopping

Work

Holiday

On the road

Cars drive on the road.

You must always wear your
seatbelt in a car.

Driving a car

Drivers make the car go where they want by using the steering wheel.

They have a horn to let other drivers know they are there.

Honk!

Honk!

11

At the garage

Drivers must put fuel into a car to make it **go**.

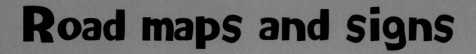

Road maps and signs

Drivers sometimes use a map to find out where they want to go.

Do you know what this sign is?

Traffic lights

Traffic lights show drivers if it is safe for them to go.

Do you know what the green light means?

Parking

Road

Car park

Big cars

Some cars are very, very big.

Have you seen a huge car like this before?

Shapes

What shapes can you see on a car journey?

wheel

traffic lights

petrol pump

Index

The end

Notes for adults

This series supports the young child's knowledge and understanding of their world and, in particular, their mathematical development. Mathematical language like *heavy/light, long/short,* and an introduction to different shapes and positional vocabulary such as *near/far,* make this series useful in developing mathematical skills. The following Early Learning Goals are relevant to the series:
• find out about, and identify, some features of living things, objects and events that they observe
• show an awareness of similarities in shapes in the environment
• observe and use positional language.

The series explores journeys and shows four different ways of travelling and so provides opportunities to compare and contrast them. Some of the words that may be new to them in **Let's Go By Car** are *journey, driver, passenger, steering wheel, pedals, horn, map, signs, fuel, petrol (and diesel),* and *limousine.* Since words are used in context in the book this should enable the young child to gradually incorporate them into their own vocabulary.

The following additional information about car journeys may be of interest:
There are many different types of car including open-topped sports cars, large people carriers, three-wheeled cars, vintage cars and very fast racing cars. They are all similar in that they have the same basic parts. Most cars have three pedals – accelerator, brake and clutch, but some cars are automatic and have only an accelerator and brake pedal.

Follow-up activities
The child could set up a road system using toys to re-enact or role play a special journey in a car. Alternatively, the child may enjoy making a record of their journey by drawing, writing or tape recording their experiences to share with others.